WHY I LIKE LAURA

Shirleyann Costigan
Illustrations by Yoshi Miyake

HAMPTON-BROWN

This is my friend Laura. Laura
always sits next to me in class.
I like Laura a lot.

She goes home with me on the
bus. We always laugh and laugh,
but that's not why I like Laura.

One time Laura found a dime.

She let me have it.
That was great, but that's not
why I like Laura.

One time Laura went to camp.

She sent me a letter.
That was great, but that's not
why I like Laura.

One time Laura's cat had
five kittens.

She let me take one.
That was great, but that's not
why I like Laura.

One time Laura got a bike.

She let me ride it.
That was great, but that's not
why I like Laura.

One time Laura had a kite.

She let me run with it.
That was great, but that's not
why I like Laura.

Let me tell you why I like Laura.
One time when I was sad she
came to sit at my side.

She said, "Paula, you are my
best friend."

She made me laugh.
That made it all fine. And <u>that's</u>
why I will always like Laura.